Goosebumps & Butterflies

written and illustrated by

Yolanda Nave

Orchard Books
New York

Orchard Books, A division of Franklin Watts, Inc.
387 Park Avenue South, New York, NY 10016

Manufactured in the United States of America
Printed by General Offset Company, Inc.
Bound by Horowitz/Rae
Book design by Mina Greenstein
The text of this book is set in 14 pt. Garamond No. 3.
The illustrations are pen and ink and watercolors, reproduced in full color.

10 9 8 7 6 5 4 3 2 1

Library of Congress Cataloging-in-Publication Data
Nave, Yolanda. Goosebumps & butterflies / by Yolanda Nave.   p.   cm.
Summary: A collection of poems about childhood fears and anxieties.
ISBN 0-531-05904-9.   ISBN 0-531-08504-X (lib. bdg.)
1. Fear—Juvenile poetry.   2. Anxiety—Juvenile poetry.   3. Children's
poetry, American.   [1. Fear—Poetry.   2. American poetry.]   I. Title.
II. Title: Goosebumps and butterflies.   PS3564.A885G6   1990
811'.54—dc20   89-48987   CIP   AC

FOR MICHAEL

GOOSEBUMPS

Goosebumps,
Vamoose bumps,
You-have-no-excuse bumps.

Ill bumps,
Chill bumps,
Just-you-wait-until bumps.

Fear bumps,
Queer bumps,
Wish-I-could-disappear bumps.

BLUEBERRY LIE

I told a lie
About blueberry pie;
I said, "I didn't do it."
I ate it all,
All by myself,
And somehow Mother knew it.

NEW BICYCLE

Sunday I got a brand-new bike;
Monday I learned how to ride;
Tuesday I went by my grandmother's house,
And to the countryside.
Wednesday I pedaled up a hill;
Thursday I reached the top;
I'll be home Friday or Saturday—
Or as soon as I learn how to stop.

GRANDPA'S GLASSES

I really didn't mean to—
It was an accident.
Maybe I should say, "I wonder
Where your glasses went?
Maybe they just disappeared,
Or slid around your head.
Maybe they're inside your beard—
Or underneath your bed.
Possibly you dropped them
In your biscuits and molasses.
Gee, Grandpa, I just can't say
Who sat upon your glasses."

ROLLER COASTER

Goosebumps on my arms and legs,
Butterflies in my belly,
Charley horses in my knees,
Oh, I don't feel so welly.

CHOIR PRACTICE

A choir is everyone singing together;

A quartet means
there are
four of us.

A trio is three;

A duet is two;

And solo means—
Wish there were more of us.

NEW HAIRDO

How do I like it?
Well, if you must ask...
I'd like it just fine, sir,
If I had a mask.

RECITAL

Which is my left foot?
Which is my right?
I cannot remember,
Try as I might.

Which toe should I point?
Which knee should I bend?
Which way should I look?
Oh, when will this end?

Which way is plié?
I'm not at all certain;
Will somebody kindly
Pull the curtain?!

SUNDAY BEST

"You can't go to church looking like that!
Why aren't you wearing your good Sunday hat?
Your petticoat's showing, your hair is a mess;
You can't wear those shoes—and look at that dress!"

But, Mother, there's something I don't understand—
Doesn't God love me just as I am?

FUNNY FACES

I can make a donkey face —
Pig faces, too!
I can make my face
Look like a kangaroo!
I can be a chimpanzee,
A monkey or giraffe!
I can even make a hyena face —
But Preacher Smith won't laugh.

WHO'S IN TROUBLE?

"All right, who let the hamster out?
Who took Benjy's dime?
Who drew pictures on the wall—
And on the floor at nap time?
Who bit Andy on the arm?
Who cut Jenny's hair?
I think it must be someone
Who's not sitting in his chair."

HIGH SLIDE

Who will catch me if I fall?
What if I land in the dirt?
Who will help me if I call—
Or cry—because I'm hurt?
Who will stop me if I slide
Too fast—and bump my head?
Who will care if I decide
To climb back down instead?

BUBBLE GUM

It's against the rule
To have gum in school,
And I hate to get in trouble.

I never thought
That I'd get caught
For blowing just one bubble.

DON'T ASK ME

Don't ask *me*
What's three plus three;
Oh please don't call my name.
Please don't say
We're going to play
Another numbers game.

What's ten minus four?
Four minus two?
I do apologize....
But to be exact,
When I subtract
I get butterflies.

What's two from eleven?
One times seven?
I really cannot tell.
If you'll excuse me,
Numbers confuse me—
But I can spell very well.

MR. BEE

I'd like to be your friend, Mr. Bee;
I'd like to sing you a song;
I'd like to finish this poem, Mr. Bee,
But really I must run along.

WHAT'S INSIDE?

What's inside
When I open wide?
Twenty-six teeth—
And butterflies.

EMILY'S PEA

When
Emily
Accidentally
Swallowed
A
Pea,
She said,
"See
What that pea
Did to
Poor little
Me?"

FISH WISH

I like this fish, but I wish I could get
A pet that's not wet and cold;
I'd rather have a pet that I
Could kiss and hug and hold.

THE GREAT OUTDOORS

There's nothing like the Great Outdoors:
The rustling of the leaves,
The sounds of frogs, and whippoorwills
And crickets in the trees;
The wind against the branches,
The night birds calling, "Hoooo";
And far, far in the distance,
Coyotes crying, "Woo-ooo."
There's nothing like the stars
And the bright moon overhead—
There's nothing quite like being safe
At home in my own bed.

ARE YOU SURE?

Are you sure that Bobo won't bite?
Are you sure he's only a pup?
Are you sure he's just being friendly?
Are you sure he won't eat me up?

SOMETHING TELLS ME

Something tells me
It's not safe to swim here;
Something tells me
I shouldn't jump in here.
Something tells me,
"Don't swim alone."
Something tells me
It's time to go home.

I BELIEVE

I believe in werewolves,
In boogeymen that bite;
I believe in spooks, and
I believe I'll turn on the light.